Jobs in Our Community

by Julie Larson

NATIONAL GEOGRAPHIC   **Hampton-Brown**

National Geographic and the Yellow Border are registered trademarks of the National Geographic Society.

National Geographic School Publishing
Hampton-Brown
www.NGSP.com

Printed in the USA.
RR Donnelley, Crawfordsville, IN.

ISBN: 978-0-7362-7995-6

13 14 15 16 17 18 19   10 9 8 7 6

Acknowledgments and credits continue on the inside back cover.

This is a doctor.

A doctor goes to a hospital.

This is a cashier.

**A cashier goes to
a shopping center.**

This is a banker.

A banker goes to a bank.

This is my teacher.
She goes to my school!